NICK SABAN AND THE PROCESS:

APPLYING THE PRINCIPLES THAT DRIVE THE GREATEST COLLEGE FOOTBALL COACH IN HISTORY TO YOUR LIFE

Presented By:

LESSONS IN LEADERSHIP INSTITUTE

LessonsInLeadership.Institute

Copyright © 2018

TABLE OF CONTENTS

Introduction

Table of Contents

Legal Notes

The Foundation of a Legacy

Life as A Coach:

Principle 1: Preparation

Principle 2: Align Yourself for Success

Principle 3: Focus on the Moment

Principle 4: Focus on What Matters

Principle 5: The Next Season Starts Yesterday

Principle 6: Adapting to the Playing Field

In His Own Words

Legal Notes

Nick Saban and the Process Presented by Lessons in Leadership Institute

© 2018 Lessons in Leadership Institute

All rights reserved. No portion of this book may be reproduced in any form without permission from the publisher, except as permitted by U.S. copyright law. For permissions contact:

BroadBasePublishing@Gmail.com

The Foundation of a Legacy

Nick Saban, the present head football coach of the University of Alabama (UA) football team, is one of the most dominant coaches in the world of football. Since his appointment in January 2007; he has taken Alabama team to an all new heights.

Nick Saban - Early Life:

Nicholas Lou Saban Jr. was born on October 31, 1951, in Fairmont, West Virginia to Nicholas and Mary Saban. His father maintained a Gulf gas station and Dairy Queen near Fairmont. Saban at his young age started working with his father.

In addition to running the Gas Station, his father, Big Nick, also coached the native Pop Warner Youth League football team and the Ida Mac Black Diamonds, where his son was the quarterback.

As he grew up Saban played at Monogah High School Lions. With Saban in the team, the Lions won the 1967 State Championship game. Further in the year in 1968, the naturally athletic Saban became famous across the state in various games such as football, basketball, and baseball.

Father's influence on Saban's Life:

Saban was so inspired by his father and his teachings that he once said that everything he does to become a champion is all because of his father and that he never spends even a single day without thinking about him.

Big Nick was the greatest mentor in his life. Since he spent most of his time with his father since his childhood, he always got an opportunity to learn from him. Whether it was sports or the life lessons, Saban learned everything from his father. His father managed to take out time from his Gulf service station to launch the Pop Warner Football. He purchased an old school bus and painted motivational messages on it. Saban Sr. used to drive the bus to the local towns to pick up the players and bring them to practice.

Saban SR was extremely supportive and fatherly towards all the children. The team he created hardly ever lost a match. The entire success of the team was the result of hard work, mental and physical strength, and self-discipline – the traits Big Nick drove into his players. He inculcated the habit of making decisions solely based on core values, taking responsibility for one's own actions and hordes of hard work!

Nick's Kids Foundation:

In the memory of his beloved father, Terry and Saban started Nick's Kids Foundation in 1998 to work as a mentor to many children. The main goal of this organization is to work together to encourage and support children while endorsing positive student causes. They help achieve these goals by spending their time arranging various events such as golf tournaments, sports, gatherings and other events to benefit the cause.

Nick's Kids Foundation has dispersed more than 8 million dollars to thousands of deserving agencies and noble causes. Some of their achievements include 16 Habitat homes and many playgrounds in schools and localities.

Nick Saban's memorable College Years:

Saban went to Kent State University on a football scholarship. He was a defensive back for the Golden Flashes team for 3 years between 1970 and 1972. During his time in the college in 1970, on May 4, 1970, to be more precise, the Ohio

National Guard killed four students following a shootout during an anti-Vietnam war demonstration. Although Saban did not witness the shooting, he saw the after math. He later said the event affected him deeply.

In Saban's senior season in the year 1972, the Golden Flashes team won the school's first and only Mid-American Conference title and later played in its first bowl game, the 1972 Tangerine Bowl.

After getting his bachelor's degree in Business from Kent State in 1973, Nick started working on a post-graduate degree. He became a graduate assistant in the football team. In 1975 he got his master's in sports administration, after which he joined the Kent State crew as the linebackers coach. The next six years, Saban worked as an assistant coach at various places such as the Syracuse University, Ohio State University, West Virginia University, and the U.S. Naval Academy.

Later in the year 1983, he was appointed as the defensive backs coach at Michigan State University, and after a year he was elevated to being the defensive coordinator.

After serving for five years there, Saban shifted to the NFL as an assistant coach of the Houston Oilers. He served there for two seasons before accepting his first job of being the head coach at the Toledo University in Ohio, where he led the Rockets to a 9-2 season and later the Mid-American Conference co-championship in the year 1990.

Moving on in his coaching career, he was hired by Bill Belichick, the new head coach of the Cleveland Browns, to be his defensive coordinator in 1991. Saban and Belichick met first in the year 1982 when Saban was a staff of the Naval Academy. Belichick's father was an assistant coach over there. In the Saban's four year tenure as the Browns staff, the team went made great progress. From allowing the highest points of 462 in the NFL, the team progressed to allowing the lowest points of 204. The team won 11 games in the year 1994 and even reached the NFL playoffs.

LIFE AS A COACH

No coach of a college football team has ruled the modern period like the legendary Nick Saban. He has been the head coach of the Alabama Crimson Tide team for the past more than 10 years. During his reign in the program, Nick has steered Alabama to six national championships.

Following are some of the accolades of his tenure as the coach:

- He is one of the only three coaches who won three national championships in a four-year period.
- He is only the second coach who won four championships in a period of seven years, in addition to Notre Dame's coach Frank Leahy.
- Saban has accumulated an amazing 127-20 record as the head coach of the Crimson Tide
- His winning rate of .864 is one of the best among all the active coaches at their current tenure.
- He carries a career record of 218-62-1.

- He is the third-fastest coach to reach the mark of 200 wins in major college football history

Let us study his life as a coach in the major places of his career:

- **Michigan State:**

Before Saban's arrived in the Michigan State in the year 1995, the Spartans were a struggling program looking for an identity. They were still recovering from recruiting violations under the coach George Perles who stepped away from the program after serving for five seasons with a record of 34-24-1.

Saban's first three years with the program did not have anything much noteworthy. The Spartans collected a record of 6-5-1 in the first year, followed up with a record of 6-6 and 7-5 in the coming seasons. The 1998 season, however, looked quite promising after a wins against Notre Dame (ranked 10) and Ohio State (ranked 1).

Saban's last season in East Lansing was his most triumphant. Michigan State finished with a record of 10-2, which was its best since 1965. This included victories against Notre Dame, Penn State, Michigan, and Ohio State. Saban then announced that he was leaving the program to join a job at the LSU.

- **LSU:**

Saban's first shift in the SEC started at LSU. He spent five seasons there as the Tigers' head coach. During that tenure of five years, Saban steered the Tigers to a record of 48-16 and two SEC championships. The high mark of his time in Baton Rouge was the Tigers defeat of the Oklahoma Sooners in the 2003 BCS Championship Game.

Saban's 48 victories were the highest ever by any LSU coach in the first five years tenure in the program. After the 2004 season, Saban resigned from LSU to take over the Miami Dolphins.

- **NFL Years**

During his time as the head coach of the Miami Dolphins the team and amassed 15-17 record. In his first season, the Dolphins started the season with a 3-7 record. Miami, however, marched to their victory of its last six games of the season to finish the season with a 9-7 record.

Entering his second season, there was a lot of enthusiasm about the future of the franchise. The team failed to meet the expectations. There were some major, yet unexpected, changes in the team as well. These changes and other factors could not make the team win. Miami finished the season with a 6-10 record, and Saban witnessed his first losing record in his career. The 2006 season was the last leap of Saban with the Dolphins. Following many public denials and rumors linking him to the opening at Alabama, Saban in due course accepted a job at the Crimson Tide in the year 2007.

- **Alabama:**

Saban, in no time, reconstructed Alabama into a dynamo with his excellent recruiting and defensive-strategy. In his third season, he headed the Crimson Tide to an amazing 14–0 record, finishing with a victory over the University of Texas in the national championship. He maintained the record with subsequent national championships in the 2011 and 2012 seasons.

Saban's accomplishments came forced the rest college football into catch up mode. To keep up with Saban's Crimson Tide schools began spending more money by upgrading their facilities and coaching salaries. This lead to the view that Saban was the best coach in college football history.

In 2016 he steered Alabama to an unbeaten regular season, where the Crimson Tide topped the Associated Press college football poll until the CFP championship games where they were upset by Clemson.

In 2017 in spite of having lost and not being a part of the SEC championship game, Alabama made the national playoffs. The team, however, proved that it was the best program of the season by easily beating Clemson in the national semi-finals, followed by the victory over the University of Georgia in the championship.

Principle 1: Preparation

The hallmark of Saban coached teams is their preparation. In almost any competitive field the team that is most prepared will win the game. Saban's record holds proof as testimony to this.

Saban had one of the most peculiar characters seen in sports. His compulsive drive explains why he is one of the most successful coaches in the history of American sports. His tenure at Alabama proved to be an unmatched reign in college football for more than five decades.

Prepare for the Battle Before It Comes – Pregame Meetings:

Nick Saban is known for being prepared for all his forthcoming games and opponents. Saban is known for his rigorous and notorious pregame meetings in which he discusses every minute and meticulous details of the approaching game.

He also made it a point to get the details of the officials involved in the game, in terms of penalties and punishments, leniencies and strictness about the happenings at the game.

Saban makes sure that his players are not affected by the psychological factors impacting their performance, thus he makes sure that all his staff and team are well prepared in advance to face all the types of scenario. He makes his players ready for every psychological and physical disturbance that they may possibly experience during the game.

For You:

Pre-Mortem: "This project failed, what killed it?"

In the medical field, it is said, "Prevention is better than cure". There is absolutely no use worrying about what has already happened, instead, preventive measures may be taken to minimize the losses.

It is quite natural that we see certain problems building up around us, yet we spare our attention to only the pressing matters.

Those things that we are ignoring now may actually become pressing in near future. If you allow issues to pile up and go wrong, they may be fatal to the project. Here in this part of the article, we have mentioned a few little ideas that may save your project from a fatal disaster.

How to Perform a Pre-Mortem in three Steps?

The concept of a Pre-Mortem is to visualize the possible factors that will lead to the failure of a project and eliminate them before the project starts. This process of pre-mortem is relatively easy yet deceptively powerful in its ability to avert disaster.

However, it is important that you follow every step in the right sequence, following the instructions carefully.

- **Step 1: Think and list down every possible problem:**

During the first hour of the pre-mortem meeting, your main job is to list down on a paper or board every single problem that has even a remote chance of occurring that would derail your project.

Don't rule out any possibility – weird, stupid or seemingly impossible. There should be no inhibitions in your thinking and imagination. The leader here should encourage his team to explore the various aspects of the same problem. The idea is to create a complete list of problems that could pop up. Make sure there is no discussion on the possible solutions at this stage.

- **Step 2: Shortlist the top problems:**

At this point, you would have an exhaustive list of problems that can potentially happen. From here you can start to eliminate problems that will etiher sort themselves out or can be handled within your current systems.

This will give you time to start establishing a short list of the most problematic events that could occur. You may start short listing based on the following attributes:

- Focus on the problems that are likely to damage your project devastatingly.
- Look at the likelihood of happening – don't waste time on things that may actually never happen!
- Eliminate the issues that you may not be able to control, such as the climatic conditions or something to do with the macro environment.

- **Step 3: Together look for Possible Solutions:**

In this step, you need to list down all the possible solutions to the various problems that have already been listed.

This is a relatively easy step, as the biggest one you have already covered – identifying the problems. Another very important point is to think of a backup plan in case the first solution doesn't work!

How Will You Deal With Things That You Can't Predict?

Problems can pop up from anywhere and sometimes the most devastating problems are the ones we don't see coming. These problems are often unforeseen and unpredicted. These problems could be related to health, finances, business, relationships, and so many. Let us go the various strategies to cope up with these unforeseen situations:

1. Be Practical:

We are often so much in our imaginary "happy go lucky" world that we feel that our current situation is going to stay like this forever. There is nothing wrong with enjoying life, but at the same time, we must understand the fact that times do change and thus be prepared to face any adversities in life.

2. Be Content:

No one on earth has everything! Rather than worrying about things that we do not have, it is better to be happy with what we have! The comparison will always make someone appear to be better and bigger.

No two people can have the same life. Hence, it is always better to look at your life in your own perspective rather than comparing with the others. This also improves our thinking and creativity, as our minds are free of negativity.

3. Don't always be in a Hurry:

This story dates back to our kindergarten days – slow and steady wins the race. Life has its own pace of giving things to us. Being in a hurry to reach a point will not let you reach their quicker; in fact, you will invite more troubles. It is better to be slow, and plan things to be prepared to face the adversaries.

4. Listen to the Gut Feeling:

Hunches are the best ways to predict the unforeseen problems. If your heart says this might go wrong, it might actually go wrong. Believe your feelings and fears, but do not be paranoid.

Principle 2: Align Yourself for Success

College Football coaching has not seen a better coach than Nick Saban. He is shrewd, smart and stupendous. Apart from the general "technical" training for the game, Saban is a great leader. We have already seen that Saban believed in being "prepared" for every possible situation in the game, as well as in life. In this part, we shall deal with a specific aspect of his training – team spirit, where all the ideas and notions aligned towards a common goal.

Everyone in Alabama's program pointing in the same direction:

Saban is an ardent decision maker – efficient to the core. It is believed that he never wasted any time even on reading menu book at the restaurant. Every day, Saban used to sit at one particular table and ate the same meal. He never wasted any time reading the menu. He would rather spend that time thinking through a new strategy. Saban strongly believed that nothing is trivial or insignificant.

What makes Saban stand apart from others is administrative protocol. He devised the plan for everything, and then a Plan B as well. He conceptualized a detailed program for his team to follow, and he is highly disciplined. Most of all Saban keeps his team focused on the proper implementation rather than the outcomes.

Prior to the arrival of Saban, the Alabama school had struggled. From being penalized for violation of NCAA rules to humiliating upsets, the school had seen a lot worse. With due credit to the methodology and nearly inhuman work ethic and energy level, Alabama has reached new heights!

Most coaches are passionate and work hard. Saban beats them all by defining the expectation for his team in every possible aspect - sports, academics, and personally. He stood with them in all conditions.

He very effectively communicated his expectations, and the expectations are so well communicated that they sink through the minds and souls of every single player in the team. Saban made the team work really hard but also knew where to stop. During every single pre-game meeting, he made sure he communicated and expressed his confidence in the members of his team.

He always used the "WE" tone – taking the blame for failures on himself, but giving the credit of performance to the entire team alone. That's what we mean when we say – all the hearts aligned in one direction. Apart from the athletic coaching, he also believed to keep the team psychologically strong so that their commitment is maintained.

Recruiting Profiles:

Tapping the right talent is unquestionably the most crucial part of the recruitment process, but the sense of commitment is equally important. The team that Saban formed in 2007, the recruitment drive forms the basis of the new fraternity of college football. The success can be accredited to Saban and his team's ability to identify prospects that could make the most of their capabilities. It is a part of his "process" which embarks with the development of a player-type model—which creates the ideal physical characteristics for specific roles and positions. Physical aspects were very important for Saban's evaluation process.

He recruited people for various roles based on their physique and physical strength. Other things such as eyesight also mattered a lot. Saban also looked for the ability to quick to change of direction and strong reflexes.

Coming to the mental abilities, mental toughness also was equally important for Saban. A persuasive character, strength and patience to follow instructions from any coaching staff and enduring mental toughness were extremely important for Saban, as these characteristics make up the mindset that is crucial to win championships. It is also important to for a player to have a strong willingness to learn and improve on a daily basis.

Saban is always very particular about position based recruitment. Usually, physically strong and rangy athletes are placed on the defense. He looks for a perfect combination of athleticism, physique, versatility and high football knowledge. Safety is another position which Saban is very particular about. Both safety positions need and have players with deep responsibility and versatility.

Saban revolutionised the running back position by giving it the due importance that has been fading in the recent past. The defensive ends players were recruited keeping in mind that they need to be heavier than others.

Breaking down the recruitment profile and process by Saban, we can say that Saban focussed on particular attributes at each position. By developing a model for what he is looking for, and ensuring they all fit together, he can ensure that the team works as a cohesive unit.

For You:

Align Everything in Your Life for Success:

Habits Aligned in the Same Direction:

Simply having the determination to win will not do any good. You must align all of your actions towards the achievement of your goals.

This is applicable to personal as well as organizational goals. Abolish all those activities that waste your time; champions set their entire focus on what they dream to achieve. They disconnect with everyone and everything that is holding them back. If you wish to achieve something, you need to set new limits for yourself and start working from this very instant.

If you aspire to be like the other successful people out there, do what they do! The comparison is not with the inferior, but with the superior. Step away from mediocrity and chase excellence. Focus on what is most important to the advancement of your life, and start working towards it.

Alter your daily routines by re-evaluating yourself before you take up any activity – ask yourself, "Is this in any way aligned with my life goals? Is this activity going to help me progress?" if the answer to all these questions is a Yes, then go ahead. If the answer is a No, then immediately quit!

Relationships Aligned to Your Goal:

To align your team towards the common organizational goals, it is important to make your team feel they are in the "big picture". The sense of togetherness, feeling important and being motivated is what drives them towards the common goal – and that is what keeps them aligned.

People who work together under proper communication, configuration, and mutual trust characterize the creative and successful team. They understand that the power of the team collectively is always greater than the sum of individual efforts. These strategies work in an excellent way to create alignment for long-term success.

Alignment is the easiest and the most efficient way to achieve organizational goals. However, some teams at times move out of alignment. This leads to internal friction, frustrations and failures leading to the derailing of the entire project. There are certain strategies through which leaders can maintain alignment in a team. We have jotted a few of them below:

1. Communicate the Objectives Clearly:

It is extremely important to clarify the exact expectations that the management has in mind, and communicate the same to the team effectively. This can only happen through periodic meetings, informal chats, reviews – and all this is extremely crucial to keeping the team aligned towards the goal. However, this continued communication does not mean you only assign the tasks, it is equally important to keep them motivated and "aligned", make them feel important and contribute to their maximum.

2. Communicate the Sense of "Belongingness":

In order to perform to our best as a team, we must inspire and elevate one another through motivation and encouragement. This is possible only when leaders empower their teammates to perform in their comfort zones, unleash their flairs, strengths, and capabilities. If each one understands the unique talents of one another, it becomes easy to "lift up" one another.

3. Communicate the management accountabilities:

There is a huge difference between designation and role. True qualities of leadership can be seen in any role and designation in an organization.

Leaders should identify the true potential of their employees and identify the leaders among them. These specific set of employees would take the necessary initiative, inspire and boost the other teammates.

4. Follow the "WE" Strategy:

A team is not a mere collection of people with varied ideas and capabilities. A team is all about trust relationships, which help in nurturing natural responsibility. When a team succeeds, the leader takes up the credit but when the team fails to deliver as expected, the blame is dumped on the team. This kills the morale of the team. The best strategy is to share the responsibility during the tough times and celebrate the victory together.

5. Don't Forget the Values, and Share Them:

Only those teams, which work towards achieving a common goal, prove to be successful in the end. Teams prove to be most effective when the individual members, along with the leader, are goal oriented and realize that they share one common goal. Apart from knowing where to go, they also work on how to get there – together. In other words, all the members of the team are aligned towards the common goal!

Principle 3: Focus on the Moment

Nick Saban is undoubtedly the most dominant head coach in the history of college football, probably of the entire American football as well. The Crimson Tide stands above all other programs as the most dominant program of the past decade.

This standard was created and established through Saban's belief in focusing on the immediate moment, which is the driving principle behind the Process.

Play Each Game as if it has a Life of its own!

For Saban, every game is a challenge, and success is not the destination but the path itself. His fierce focus is continuously on the task of maintaining Alabama's position at the top of the world of college football.

Once naïve and affected by the external expectations, now Saban is more of a person who takes the game as his own personal venture and treats the game as if it has a life of its own – he gives due attention, respect and love to the game!

When Saban was at the Michigan State University, his approach towards the game was totally different. For him, the game was only about winning, and this elicited constant pressure on him. This approach towards the game made him feel stressed, and so it affected the team in the same way.

He said it was before their upset over Ohio State where his approach changed forevet. In this game he told the players to not worry about the end result because upsetting the Buckeyes seemed like such a monumental task. Instead he told them to focus one play at a time and to win each indidivdual play. The result was one of the biggest upsets in Michigan State history.

As he took over the LSU program, he adopted the philosophy that they are going to play one game at a time, in a way that the game has a life of its own. He expanded this to off field development as well. This resulted in better mindset and productivity, and in turn, resulted in better output.

The battle:

Now the fight wasn't with the competitors to win the battle on the football ground but within himself. He wished to conquer his senses and gain control over his mind, rather than controlling the external factors.

Saban strongly believed that the obstacles on one's path only make him stronger and better as a human, and as an athlete. They are never meant to impede an individual, but to improve him. This approach has made Saban quite a lot like a duck - quiet on the surface, paddling frantically below under the water.

Saban was very particular about the way his team played football, but also how they treated other people. He believed that his team must show high levels of compassion for other people and have strong and genuine helping tendencies.

Another element of life that Saban believes to be very dangerous is Contentment – which always seems to accompany success. Once you feel complacent, your desire to grow and improve ends that very moment. Contentment leads to a deliberate disregard for doing the right things.

In an effort to fight the tendency to get content with the past successes and events, Saban has created a culture in his coaching which developed the right leadership skills in the individuals at various levels.

Even though Saban devotes a large part of his time planning and thinking about the upcoming game rather than thinking about the previous one, he spares some of the time on himself too.

For Your Life

No Bad Days:

How many of you believe that happiness is just a state of mind; that one can be happy if he decides to stay so, and that "bad days" are just products of your own thoughts?

Many of us can easily get bogged down. If our day doesn't go according to our expectations or plans, we simply become disturbed and upset. What do we do when we encounter such a situation? Just shrug off and say "oh it was a bad day". It is extremely easy for someone to blame the day and decide to start anew the next day. But just imagine, is it worth to call a day bad just because one thing didn't happen your way?

Consider the magnitude of damage this would do to your productivity, mood and relationships. One bad thing per day for a month for an entire year – potentially you have wasted so time focusing one petty issue, which would not even matter a few days after! Being positive and open to new things is the solution to these kinds of problems. Remember, there are no bad days unless you CREATE one!

The attitude and mindset with which you wake up every morning is the deciding factor in making a day good or bad. Get up with a smile, and with the attitude that "today I am positive, and will let only positive things to happen to me today", we are sure there are not going to be any bad days.

"No bad days" is just an art of living; a concept; a practice that we all need to follow. If you strongly believe that there are no bad days, there are not going to be any bad days. Remember, their can only be bad moments, but all of those bad moments are just passing clouds. Follow positivity and spread positivity to make the "bad days' of others into good days!

Stay in the moment:

How many of you have heard the saying – yesterday is history, tomorrow is the mystery and today is a gift, that is why it is called the "present". The only moment, which you have control on, is the present moment.

But most of us waste our present moment either thinking about the past or worrying about what the future holds for us. It could be the reverse as well – we keep on reliving the old sunny memories or daydreaming about the uncertain happiness supposedly waiting for you, somewhere in your future.

This is not healthy; the best lifestyle is to live in the moment. Moreover, we will tell you the easiest ways to do so. Here we go:

1. **Don't Multi-task if that stresses you:**

Taking up one task and completing it properly and perfectly not only gives you pleasure but also enables you to live in the present moment. It is as simple as only eating while you are eating, not watching TV. Alternatively, not having the Smartphone at home while you are having a conversation with your partner.

2. Patience is the Key:

Hurrying on doing a task would only fetch you more tension and uncertainty of results. If you do the same thing with a little patience and love, your stress levels will be the lot lower and you can visualize the results as the events unfold before your eyes.

Do your tasks at an unperturbed and calm pace. This certainly does not mean that your work will be completed later than expected. This would only mean that you will be able to live at present with the stern focus on the task at hand.

3. Live Your Role:

Life is all about role plays. When you are sitting with your child assisting her with her homework, you are her teacher. "Be there", while you are performing a task. This habit is the most important while doing things which may divert you to past or future.

4. Be Selectively Absorbent:

Don't be a sponge that absorbs every single thing that you come across. While browsing through Facebook if you come across an old lady who is toothless and probably homeless, don't start imagining yourself in her position and pile up the stress on your head. If you start taking in everything in your head, it will become too hard for you to concentrate on the task at hand. This is a big hindrance for you to stay in the present moment, as you tend to be dragged into the vicious cycle of negative thoughts.

5. Self -Control and Self- Realization:

There will be moments where you are forced to think about the past or worry about the future. Voluntarily or involuntarily, you are somehow dragged into the times that are playing inside our heads. All the tips mentioned above may make it easier to stay in the present moment, but there is something more which is required to keep yourself and your thoughts fixed on the present. You need to have discipline to stay at present. Unless you have that determination and willpower to overcome your weakness and strive to improve your thinking process, you can never succeed.

Principle 4: Focus on What Matters

Nick Saban is not only a great coach but also a great mentor. He emphasized on the improvement of the real-life aspects such as compassion, helping tendency and mutual respect as much as he did on the technical aspects of the game. He lives in "present", ignoring the clutter around.

Ignore the Clutter:

Nick Saban clearly understands it is not possible to control the expectations of the people who wish to see Alabama win the national championship title. These expectations and disturbances, according to him, are "clutter". He is never worried about winning the national title, at the same time he does not want his team also to worry about it. Several times he has snubbed the reporters and asked them not to mention about the championship or the chances of winning it. He emphasized only on the game, believing that this game is the only thing that ever matters! In fact, Saban could easily ignore the so-called "clutter", but only if the reporters never brought the topic.

Saban never even uttered the word "national championship", as confirmed by his team members.

This philosophy of Saban was so well handled and carried forward through his team that Alabama is now accustomed to handling the hypes and gossip that comes with their dominant tradition. Alabama was now much more experienced in handling propaganda and has mostly navigated away from all the troubles off the field.

For Your Life:

What Really Makes Difference?

Someone has very rightly said that life is too short to hold on to grudges and material pleasures. Therefore, it is better to only focus on what really matters and let go of what does not matter at all. Have you ever noticed that those who have fewer material possessions are the lot happier than those who have a lot of those? Those people who spend more time in earning experiences than earning money are happier than those who focus on money and material possessions.

Our most precious possessions are not our material possessions such as smartphones, high-end TVs, modern cars, or massive homes. The actual precious possessions are our purpose in life, our time, our health, and the most valued among all are our relationships.

Purpose: Purpose refers to the reason for our existence. Our purpose transcends our profession, connections, and our attitude towards life. Our purpose in life actually shapes our life. Our purpose makes us hold on to our beliefs when things get tough.

Time: Have you ever observed that all of us have got the same 24 hours, but why is it that some of us struggle for the time even to do the basic things whereas some of us accomplish a lot and still manage to have the "me" time. The answer lies in the very fact that we need to prioritize our activities – make the right choices. It is important that we understand what is important in the present and accomplish that task in hand.

Well-being: In the race to earn money and accomplish other things in life, we often forget the other most important thing – our health.

Health is the one thing that we take for granted most often. We often miss out to indulge in some physical activity or exercise to maintain our good health. We ignore the healthy diet and satisfy our momentary cravings. Similarly, we often forget we should lead a stress-free life in order to maintain sound mental health.

Relationships: Our poor relationships are often the product of our own lifestyle. While going after money and other material obsessions, we forget that our most precious possessions are our relationships – the people we live with! Our relationships are our core; our substance that marks our lives. We need to cherish them with all the heart and attention which they really are worthy of.

If It Doesn't Matter It Doesn't Matter!

The mind is the master of our body. It controls our thinking, our desires and our priorities. It allows the negative thoughts to dominate us, or the positive thoughts to shape our personalities. The mind is not so easy to control. No wonder how strangely we change our moods – we keep oscillating between good and bad, fun and solitude, wisdom and stupidity!

We often tend to ignore magnificent things, thinking of them to be petty. In addition, sometimes we magnify trivial things. It is the entire mind's game. There are advantages also, though. When the mind chooses not to 'mind' negative and other destructive emotions such as grief, vengeance and sorrow, it makes us feel that it really doesn't matter!

Have you noticed that there are days everything seems to be trivial and we feel all happy-go-lucky, but there are other days when even a small and irritates us! The same situation renders too extremely opposite reactions from us in two different situations.

Why does all this happen? Where does this kind of "dual character" take birth? Simply based on the impulse of our mind, we react to different situations or different people in different ways at different times. We create our own perceptions and limitations in our mind about different things, and about things and their limit of acceptability.

Actually, our acceptance or negation of things depends a lot on our mood.

We must understand that unless we clearly establish the boundaries in our mind, it is going to continue to be shillyshallied and keep creating unnecessary disturbances and confusions. All this would only lead to constant feelings of being disturbed, aggravated and stressed. Once you decide not to give your precious attention to anything trivial, then it will just stop bothering you. It is all how to train your mind – if you train it to mind, it will mind; if you train it to let go, I will let go – ultimately resulting in happiness!

Principle 5: The Next Season Starts Yesterday

Football is a game that tends to evolve over time. There is no other coach in the history of American college football coaching that has impacted college football as much as the legendary Nick Saban.

Saban is known for his tactics in getting the getting the best out of the team – in terms of performance on the field and performance off the field. The entire credit, of course, cannot be taken by Saban.

The National Championship Cost Us A Month in Recruiting:

Accept it or not, Saban is the notorious mind behind the Crimson Tide. There definitely has to be a reason why the Crimson Tide team is consistently picked to be the top team in college football.

Saban is one of those most effective people who devise a special formula that works in their personal life as beautifully as in their professional life – a discipline that defines their way of life.

Saban has also devised a specific formula for his recruiting process, and this new philosophy has revolutionised the American college football. Saban's technique of recruiting is quite similar to that of the drafting strategy of Bill Belichick in the NFL. This method can be broken down into the following:

- **Depth:**

Saban works on the simple approach while recruiting his team. Saban calculates the needs of his team at present, also keeping in mind what the team might need a few years down the line. He keeps in fact in mind that he must have a strong and suitable replacement should somebody leave the team. Every member of the team gets the precious opportunity to train under the guidance of great coaches, observe great players, get the necessary playing and practice period and gradually showcase their enormous talent on the field.

- **Mold:**

Saban focuses on finding recruits with the ability to be both versitale and adapt to the team structure and culture they will experience at the University of Alabama. Saban also focuses.

Saban draws the conclusion that when he recruits people with specific traits for specific positions, he is more successful. Thus, he makes sure that he recruits players who fit into those positions or the moulds. Nick Saban has also forced other SEC colleges and schools to follow his recruiting technique.

Hatred of Complacency:

Success has always been like a continuous journey for Saban, and he has always been on the lookout for things, situations and people he can learn from – both professionally and personally. Saban was never satisfied – for good reasons of course. He never stopped at his successes or took rest at a point. Most of us like to sit back and cherish our success, which is definitely deadly and detrimental to our lives. Nick Saban never rests on his success or feels complacent about the achievements of his team. Every victory opens doors for new opportunities and challenges, and challenges bring the best out of an individual.

People often felt surprised, often complained too, about how non-expressive Saban is. Terms such as unnerving, unsmiling, and unfriendly are the terms used for him. People call him "joyless", as he never expressed his happiness even after winning a championship title. However everyone has their own way of celebrating success! For Saban the joy is in the success. With every successful match, he starts working on how to make the upcoming game a success rather than wasting time on celebrating his previous victory.

For You:

Do Not Rest On Success:

Does a Hollywood star retire after getting the Oscars, thinking that he has achieved everything that he ever dreamt of? While they might celebrate some of these successes with some extravagant vacations and short breaks, there is always the focus on the next step? Successful people never rest on success; they rather skip every opportunity of resting and take up every chance to make themselver better than before.

Have you ever tried to figure out what keeps bringing successful people back to work every single time? It is nothing but their passion to succeed more. It is their thirst to excel and improve with every opportunity. They see the passion in their work, not boredom or burden.

There might be times when you would feel a little "bored "or "tired" of what you are doing at present. After spending a considerable time in your present profession, you might think you have had enough. This is quite natural. So what do you do then? That's where your hobby comes into the picture! If you feel tired of playing a particular game, just sit back and think what is the second most passionate thing in your life – fishing? Or is it Music? Or maybe painting? That's what successful people do – look for alternatives when you actually feel you are done!

Success is all about striking the perfect balance between motivation and action. You do not have to burn yourself up to get the desired success. At the same time, you cannot afford to just sit and relax all day. In short, you can say that success does not come from staying passive and resting on your achievements; it rather comes from planning and achieving your next laurel.

Using Success to Build More Success:

If we ask you, what success means to you, we are sure you would use the dictionary definition and tell us "when you achieve something that you have been working on?" For some success is all about the material possessions he or she has attained in life, and for some, it is all about the "self-actualization".

Everyone has a dream – and we keep fighting the whole life to achieve what we dream of. Some dreams change through the course of life. Some of them come true and some do not. While everyone will experience failure it is critical that we do not stop trying and dreaming of the next success. We never stopped trying to be better or trying to do better. Why should we stop when we succeed once?

Immediate success and constant success:

There is a difference between being successful and being constantly successful. Once you achieve something, you become successful. However, in order to be constantly successful, you need to keep achieving and over-achieving your targets. You will be required to keep challenging your so-called limits and constantly be on the run to challenge your imaginary limitations.

Remember, obstacles are not mountains; they are mere speed bumps – they may slow you down for a while, but they do not have the strength to stop your full momentum. This can be done only if you develop self-confidence and have faith in your dreams. Accepting momentary defeats with grace and intelligence and learning from the mistakes of the past can only make you stronger and you can evolve into a new YOU – new, better and improved version of you.

The key to having a successful life is to understand that success is not the destination – instead it is the path on which we travel! Success is the stepping-stone to the next chapter of life, which gives you a new opportunity to learn and improve. Every step is an opportunity to challenge yourself and your capabilities. Walk the path you have never seen, and chase the new target. Dare to dream all over again, and start working towards achieving it.

Remember – every day is a new opportunity – make the most of it. Treat every success as a stepping-stone to go to the next level. Do not be bogged down with momentary failures; these are just passing clouds – like Charlie Chaplin said, "Nothing is permanent; not even our troubles".

So dream more, achieve more and succeed more – that is what life is all about!

Principle 6: Adapting to the Playing Field

Saban is a live example of how to adapt to the changes on and off the field; he knew that adapting to changes is the most important key to success. As much as he believed in planning and being prepared he has adapted to the changes in the game over the past 20 years. After all, the game is all about evolving and improving.

Utilizing a Running Quarterback and Up Tempo Offenses:

Saban has seen the game and the team evolve over the past 5 years - both offensive as well as defensive aspects. Saban believes that the game has dramatically evolved in the course of five years.

The most prominent and evident changes that have taken place at Alabama are seen on the offense.

Saban began to use mobile quarterbacks which was a huge shift from his traditional pocket style passers that he had relied on throughout his career. In addition he moved to an up-tempo, spread based offense that he had previously blasted in the media. Saban's misapprehension was the safety of the players, and he feels that the rules permit the offences to play very fast, involving too many moves in shorter time.

But yes, there is one thing that has never changed in the past 5 years – and that is Nick Saban's habit of winning every game he is involved in. His thought process took a turn around after losing back to back against Auburn and Oklahoma in 2013.

Saban made certain refined changes on the defensive side. He took intensive efforts to take in players who could play three continuous downs and play better against all the spread, tempo based offenses.

For You:

Stay up to the current trends in your sector:

Change is the only constant, and any improvement ever made is only for the betterment of the organization. Whenever there is a change in the industry, it is important that you walk in line with the changes. Staying updated with the latest happenings in your industry will keep you growing. In order to keep yourself updated, you can follow a few very simple methods. Here are some of them for your ready reference:

1. Research Reports: Many times, the industry experts carry out original research and compile their inferences in a report. Take out some time to go through these; they are sure to enlighten you.

2. Follow the Publications: Do you belong to that category of people who do not want to read long and boring reports? Then the next best option is to go through the fortnightly or monthly publications that contain the gist of the matter! Usually, the articles in those publications are based on the data from the original reports and serve as more readable summaries.

3. Make "Good Friends": Another way of staying updated about the industry changes is to surround yourself with people who practice the habits mentioned in the above two points. Converse with these peers about what their company might be doing with the research.

4. Stay in Touch with Advisors: Always keep a group of friends, colleagues or relatives that can advise you on formal and informal matters concerning various industry perspectives.

5. Social Media: It is not always about sharing pictures and updating status messages. Various social media platforms such as Twitter and Facebook are often loaded with latest updates about the industry and the market. You just have to subscribe to the newsfeeds of your choice and interest.

6. Change is Not All That Bad: Like it is said in many places – change is the only constant. The more you adapt to the changing environments and address to industry developments in a more open and modern way, you are more likely to keep yourself updated with the other developments related to the industry.

How can you adapt what you do to what is successful?

We, humans, have a very bad habit of procrastinating and taking things for granted unless something serious comes up! There are certain habits that would form almost instantly but will endure permanently. The simple example is how we don't really get down to reducing weight unless the doctor says that we might end up in some really serious ailment if we don't shed some pounds. This thought of "something very serious" dominates us so intensely and frightens us so badly that we immediately start doing everything that is required for weight loss. In short, we change our "habits" into something that would become the art of our living for the rest of our lives.

How are these habits actually formed? And how would you develop a new habit that would lead you to success? We have devised simple methods to help you in this regard:

- The decision to forming a new habit needs to be strong and firm.
- Discipline is the key – don't allow yourself to take pity or give excuses for "exceptions".
- If you are not confident in yourself, just tell others that you are going to change a

particular habit or behavior — the fear of being watched is often enough to keep your discipline.
- Keep visualizing yourself already performing the new habit or behavior. Your subconscious mind will train you to become what you wish to become.
- Keep telling yourself that you to have to do this!
- Keep practicing!!
- You deserve a treat if you successfully perform the activity. Incentivize your activities to keep yourself motivated.

In His Own Words

On Discipline

- "Character is what you do when no one else is watching."
- "Discipline is not punishment. Discipline is changing someone's behavior."
- "There are two pains in life. There is the pain of discipline and the pain of disappointment. If you can handle the pain of discipline, then you'll never have to deal with the pain of disappointment."
- "Do the right thing. It's that simple. Do the right thing when the right thing is not popular. Do the right thing when no one else is around. Do the right thing when temptation tells you otherwise. Do the right thing all the time."
- "The process is really what you have to do day in and day out to be successful, we try to define the standard that we want everybody to sort of work toward, adhere to, and do it on a consistent basis. And the things that I talked about before, being

responsible for your own self-determination, having a positive attitude, having great work ethic, having discipline to be able to execute on a consistent basis, whatever it is you're trying to do, those are the things that we try to focus on, and we don't try to focus as much on the outcomes as we do on being all that you can be."

- "We create a standard for how we want to do things and everybody's got to buy into that standard or you really can't have any team chemistry. Mediocre people don't like high-achievers and high-achievers don't like mediocre people."
- "Eliminate the clutter and all the things that are going on outside and focus on the things that you can control with how you sort of go about and take care of your business. That's something that's ongoing, and it can never change."
- "If you don't get result-oriented with the kids, you can focus on the things in the process that are important to them being successful."

- "When you invest your time, you make a goal and a decision of something that you want to accomplish. Whether it's make good grades in school, be a good athlete, be a good person, go down and do some community service and help somebody who's in need, whatever it is you choose to do, you're investing your time in that."
- "When you play against good people, that's when you focus your concentration. Your sense of urgency to be disciplined in your execution all become more critical. Sometimes you get away with doing things not quite right against lesser competition, but when you play against real good people that's when it shows up."
- "One thing about championship teams is that they're resilient. No matter what is thrown at them, no matter how deep the hole, they find a way to bounce back and overcome adversity."
- "We all have anxiety about things. We all have little insecurities, but eventually you have to face your fears if you want to be

successful, and everybody has some fear of failure."

On Improvement

- "Success doesn't come from pie-in-the-sky thinking. It's the result of consciously doing something each day that will add to your overall excellence."
- "The good is enough attitude is not what we're looking for, we have got to use every opportunity to improve individually so we can improve collectively"
- "Champions are rare. Everybody has some chance, some opportunity to change and improve, but not everybody takes advantage. Be somebody who does."
- "Mediocre people don't like high achievers, and high achievers don't like mediocre people."
- "It's not human nature to be great. It's human nature to survive, to be average and do what you have to do to get by. That is normal. When you have something good happen, it's the special people that can stay focused and keep paying attention to detail, working to get better and not being satisfied with what they have accomplished."

- "Becoming a champion is not an easy process… It is done by focusing on what it takes to get there and not on getting there."
- "I think everybody should take the attitude that we're working to be a champion, that we want to be a champion in everything that we do. Every choice, every decision, everything that we do every day, we want to be a champion."
- "I'm tired of hearing all this talk from people who don't understand the process of hard work-like little kids in the back seat asking 'Are we there yet?' Get where you're going 1 mile-marker at a time."
- "The more one emphasizes winning, the less he or she is able to concentrate on what actually causes success."
- "When people have success, one of two things happen. They either get really satisfied and want to keep thinking about it and talking about what they did, or the success becomes a little addictive, and it makes them want to keep having more."

- "What makes Freddy Krueger such a horrible character? What makes him scare you to death? You can't get rid of the guy. He never goes away."
- "There is no continuum for success. Focus on the progress, not the results."
- "There is no continuum for success. Focus on the progress, not the results."
- "Every choice, every decision, everything we do everyday, we want to be a champion."
- "I don't care what you did yesterday. If you're happy with that, you have bigger problems."

On Leadership

- "Great leaders are not always popular."
- "Some of the great leaders in history were not adored, but respected. My advice to leaders—stop trying to please everyone and do what you believe is best."
- "Baseball manager Casey Stengel once quipped, "The secret of managing is to keep the guys who hate you away from the guys who are undecided."
- "Teaching is the ability to inspire learning."

Made in the USA
San Bernardino, CA
12 September 2019